GREAT
BUILDING
FEATS

THE
PANTHEON

LESLEY A. DuTEMPLE

Lerner Publications Company
Minneapolis

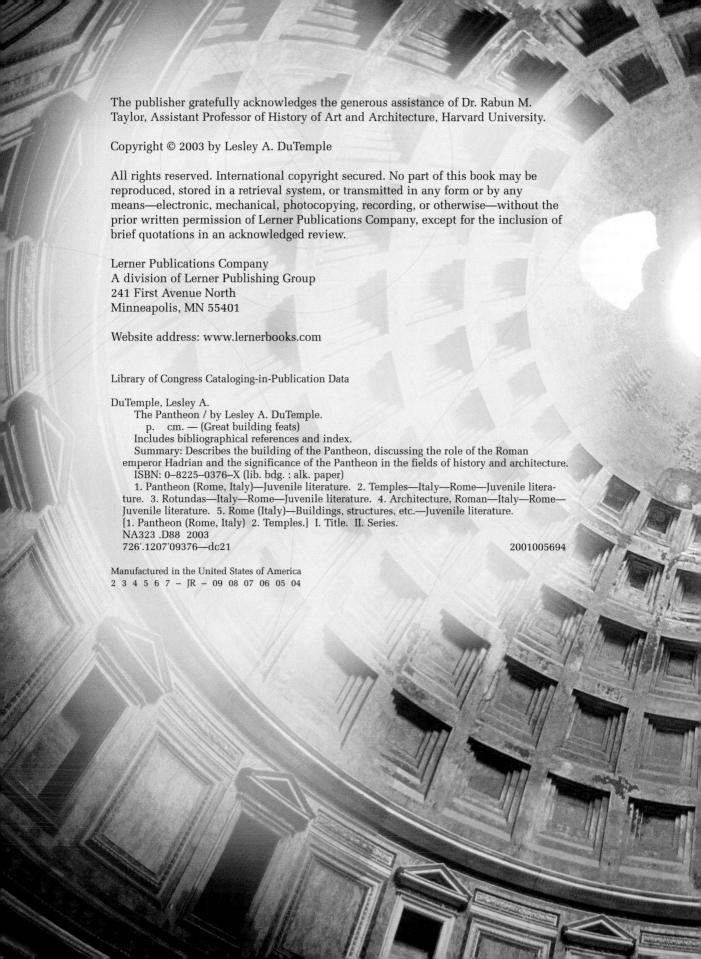

The publisher gratefully acknowledges the generous assistance of Dr. Rabun M. Taylor, Assistant Professor of History of Art and Architecture, Harvard University.

Lerner Publications Company
A division of Lerner Publishing Group
241 First Avenue North
Minneapolis, MN 55401

Website address: www.lernerbooks.com

Library of Congress Cataloging-in-Publication Data

DuTemple, Lesley A.
    The Pantheon / by Lesley A. DuTemple.
      p.   cm. — (Great building feats)
    Includes bibliographical references and index.
    Summary: Describes the building of the Pantheon, discussing the role of the Roman emperor Hadrian and the significance of the Pantheon in the fields of history and architecture.
    ISBN: 0–8225–0376–X (lib. bdg. : alk. paper)
    1. Pantheon (Rome, Italy)—Juvenile literature. 2. Temples—Italy—Rome—Juvenile literature. 3. Rotundas—Italy—Rome—Juvenile literature. 4. Architecture, Roman—Italy—Rome—Juvenile literature. 5. Rome (Italy)—Buildings, structures, etc.—Juvenile literature.
    [1. Pantheon (Rome, Italy) 2. Temples.] I. Title. II. Series.
    NA323 .D88 2003
    726'.1207'09376—dc21
                                                                                          2001005694

Manufactured in the United States of America
2 3 4 5 6 7 – JR – 09 08 07 06 05 04

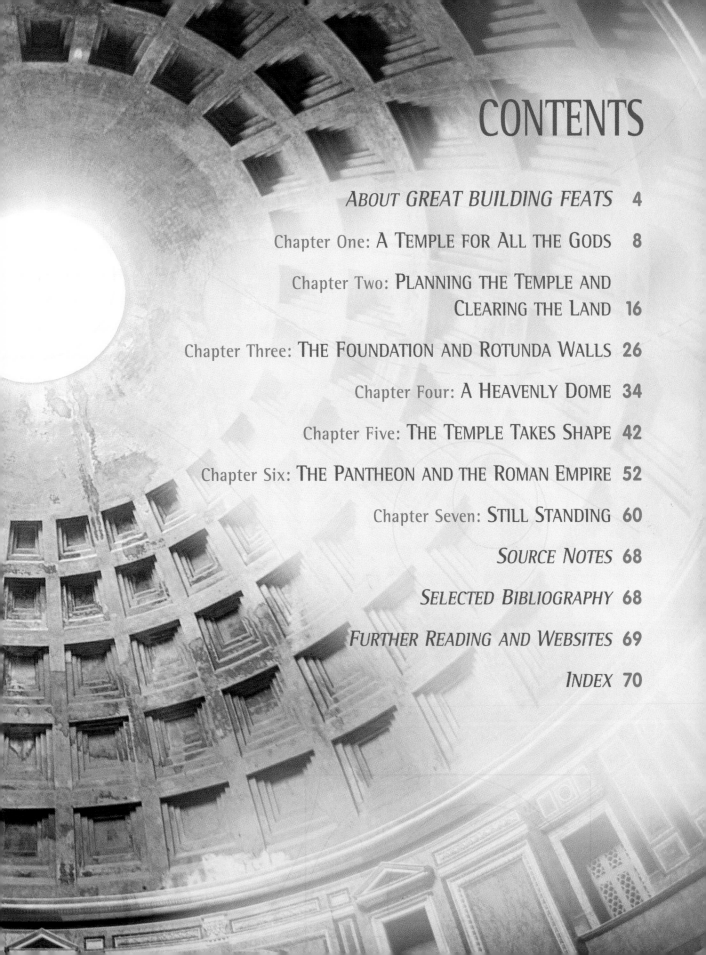

CONTENTS

ABOUT GREAT BUILDING FEATS

HUMANS HAVE LONG SOUGHT to make their mark on the world. From the ancient Great Wall of China to the ultramodern Channel Tunnel linking England and France, grand structures reveal how people have tried to express themselves and better their lives.

Great structures have served a number of purposes. Sometimes they met a practical need. For example, the New York City subway system made getting around a huge city easier. Other structures reflected religious beliefs. The Taj Mahal in northern India is one of the most beautiful and costly tombs in the world. Sometimes we can only guess at the story behind a structure. The purpose of Stonehenge in England eludes us, and perhaps it always will.

This book is one in a series of books called

The Pantheon, with its massive concrete dome, is a major landmark in modern Rome.

Great Building Feats. Each book in the series takes a close look at one of the most amazing building feats around the world. Each of them posed a unique set of engineering and geographical problems. In many cases, these problems seemed nearly insurmountable when construction began.

More than a compilation of facts, the Great Building Feats series not only describes how each structure was built but also why. Each project called forth the best minds of its time. Many people invested their all in the outcome. Their lives are as much a part of the structure as the earth and stone used in its construction.

Finally, each structure in the Great Building Feats series remains a dynamic feature of the modern world, still amazing users and viewers as well as historians.

THE PANTHEON

When the Pantheon was completed in about A.D. 128, it must have seemed awesome to any Roman who walked into it. The Pantheon's domed ceiling stretches 142 feet (43 meters) across—the largest dome anyone had ever built. The dome has no support beams or columns to hold it up in the middle. Just getting it to stay up was a remarkable feat for ancient builders.

The Pantheon was such an influential building that architects sketched it and studied its every detail for centuries after its construction.

But the Pantheon was also symbolically important. Built by the emperor Hadrian, the building was designed as a temple for all the Roman gods. Nearly perfect in its shape, the vast dome represented the heavens, which were seen by Romans as an enormous sphere. At the same time, the Pantheon served as one of the emperor's official places of business. Hadrian wanted people to see the heavens (which were ruled by the gods) and the Roman Empire (which was ruled by Hadrian himself) represented in the same place. The Pantheon's message was clear: the empire was huge, watched over and protected by the gods.

The Pantheon's use of other architectural elements also would have been stunning to the ancient Romans. Building domes was not new, but combining a domed cylinder with a traditional, Greek temple entrance, as the Pantheon did, *was* new. The combination was an innovation that changed architecture permanently. Even in modern times, a domed rotunda with a temple front is one of the most prominent building designs in existence.

Just as the design of the Pantheon has survived into modern times, so too has the building itself. The Pantheon still stands in Rome, Italy, where it was built nearly two thousand years ago. And it stands in very nearly the same condition as it did when it was built. Its structural integrity is remarkable, considering that even our strongest modern concrete buildings may stand for only a few hundred years. Many questions about the Pantheon still tease modern scholars. A dome that matched the Pantheon in size was not completed until 1446, well over a thousand years after completion of the Pantheon. How did the ancient Romans raise such a large dome, using none of the gas-powered machinery or other building advantages of modern times? Amazingly, the ancient Romans erected the Pantheon in only about ten years. How did they do it so quickly?

Our answers to these questions are incomplete. Few written records remain from that era, and much of what does survive may not be entirely accurate. Although we may never know the whole story, we can continue to study the building itself in search of answers. Modern technology, such as X rays and computers, is helping us to learn more about how the Pantheon was built. Selective excavation is also uncovering clues about how the Pantheon's architect solved some difficult engineering problems in unique ways.

The Pantheon's secrets still intrigue us, and its beauty and symbolism still inspire. And what we know of its story—how it was built, and why—still fascinates us.

Chapter One
A Temple for All the Gods

A.D. 117–118

When Hadrian received news in A.D. 117 that his adoptive father, the emperor Trajan, had died, he was an officer in the Roman army, stationed far from the city of Rome. Although Hadrian would become the new emperor of the Roman Empire, he took his time getting back to Rome, traveling through the provinces of the empire and meeting with soldiers. These visits took more than a year. But they were a smart move on Hadrian's part.

Above: This relief shows Hadrian entering Rome, greeted at the gates by Roma, the goddess of Rome, and others.

Right: The Romans spread news and recorded their history by stamping images on coins. This coin shows Hadrian addressing his troops in England.

He needed to establish his authority as the emperor and to demonstrate concern for his soldiers.

As Hadrian and his traveling companions finally approached Rome, many people made their way up the road outside the city to greet him. Some people walked. Others cantered along on fine horses or rode in chariots. Senators, police officers, soldiers, and citizens—rich and poor alike—all came out to see Hadrian. There were supporters as well as critics of the new ruler. The mint at Rome had already made coins commemorating his return.

Inside the city, Hadrian would have seen a large burned area in the Campus Martius, a huge public gathering area in the western part of the city. The Pantheon, a temple located there, had been struck by lightning during Trajan's reign and burned to the ground. Built by a man named Marcus Agrippa in 25 B.C., the Pantheon had been a temple for all the Roman gods. Its name came from the Greek words *pan,* meaning "all," and *theos,* meaning "gods." This was the second time the Pantheon had burned. The people of Rome had been without this important building for several years.

For Hadrian, the idea of rebuilding the Pantheon may have come as rapidly as the lightning that had destroyed the temple. The Roman Empire was at the height of its powers. Life for the Romans was, for the most part, prosperous and safe. A newly designed Pantheon, perfect in its construction and stunning in its beauty, could reflect the symmetry and power of the Roman Empire.

THE EMPIRE

Hadrian was the fourteenth emperor of the Roman Empire. The empire had been getting larger for many years and covered most of the known world. Because of his empire's power, Hadrian was the most important person alive.

Before Rome was ruled by emperors, it had been a republic. Elected officials headed the government, and the Senate was the most powerful governmental body. During the 300s B.C., Rome fought with other civilizations on the peninsula that is present-day Italy. By 275 B.C., Rome ruled most of the peninsula. The republic began to expand outside of the peninsula during the 200s and 100s B.C. In 49 B.C, a Roman leader named Julius Caesar led an army to Rome, his own city, provoking a civil war that eventually made him the dictator of the Roman world. *Dictator* was a term used during the republic to indicate a leader with special temporary powers. Many people believed that Caesar's power was illegal. When he tried to expand his power by making himself dictator for life, he was assassinated. Civil war broke out again, and Caesar's adopted son, Octavian, managed to defeat his rivals and take control in 27 B.C.

Octavian changed his name to Augustus, which means "exalted" in Latin, the language of Rome. He avoided the title emperor. He preferred to be called princeps, which means "first citizen." Whatever his title, Augustus had tremendous power. Caesar had never controlled the Senate, but Augustus was able to fill the Senate with his supporters. Caesar had controlled only a few legions of the army, but Augustus

Right: The Senate often met in a place called the Forum.
Opposite: Augustus as princeps

commanded almost the entire army. Caesar had controlled only the few provinces where he had military power, but Augustus controlled virtually all of the provinces.

No one—not even Caesar himself—believed Caesar's dictatorship would survive his death. But it quickly became clear that Augustus's legal, recognized form of power would last. Before Augustus died in A.D. 14, he arranged to have his adopted son succeed him. This established the tradition of an emperor choosing his successor—usually another family member or a favorite, someone adopted for the occasion.

In practice if not in title, Augustus had become Rome's first emperor. Over the years, the authority of the Roman emperors grew. And so did the Roman Empire.

EMPERORS WHO BUILT

The Senate oversaw the public treasury and helped the emperor decide how tax money should be spent. But taxes weren't the only money used to fund projects in the empire. Nearly every Roman emperor built at least one public structure—a building or a freestanding arch or column—with his own money. It was an emperor's obligation to use his

NOT SO HIGH

Emperors were not the only people who built structures in Rome. Private architects also built, and some built very tall buildings. Sometimes architects tried to outdo each other by putting up taller and taller buildings. But Emperor Augustus worried that the tall buildings were spoiling Rome's appearance. He was also concerned about safety. Cramped, overly tall buildings were liable to collapse. Fire was another danger. To preserve the beauty and safety of the city, he issued a decree forbidding the construction of buildings higher than 60 feet (18 meters).

wealth and influence to sponsor art and social goods. The structures he built also served as tangible reminders that the emperor was generous and that the empire was prosperous and great.

Sometimes emperors built structures to commemorate a specific event, such as winning a particular battle. Still other times they built buildings for entertainment. Theaters, stadiums, public baths, and pools kept people happy.

The Romans worshiped many gods, and most of these gods had their own temples. The Romans believed that the gods required strong allegiance. If things were going badly—if a river was flooding or battles were being lost—it was because the gods were angry. In that case, people tried to make the gods happy again. If things were going well, the people offered thanks. If an emperor was grateful for a success, or if he wanted to gain divine favor, he might build an entire temple to a particular god or goddess to thank him or her. Augustus felt that Mars, the god of war, had helped him avenge the murder of his adoptive father, Julius Caesar. So Augustus built a temple to thank him.

Roman emperors themselves were worshiped almost like gods. In fact, when a capable and respected Roman emperor died, he was deified—proclaimed to be a god. After Augustus died in A.D. 14, the Senate deified him. Temples were built to honor him throughout the empire. Special priests, called Augustales, were appointed. The Romans worshiped Augustus, who had been a good leader. But many didn't believe he was really a god like Jupiter or Mars. When they wanted help, they prayed to their "real" gods. Worshiping a dead emperor was a way to show loyalty to the empire.

Hadrian's father, Trajan, was deified after he died, making Hadrian the son of a god. Because Hadrian was now related to the gods, rebuilding the Pantheon—a temple where all Roman gods were worshiped—may have seemed very important to him.

HADRIAN'S EMPIRE

When Hadrian became emperor, the Romans ruled all of present-day Italy, Greece, Spain, France, England, and Turkey, as well as large parts of eastern Europe, the Middle East, and most of Egypt and northern Africa. Trajan's policy had been to expand the empire. But Hadrian thought the empire had expanded enough. He shifted the army's focus away from attacking and toward keeping the empire safe and enforcing

The shaded area shows land controlled by the Romans when Hadrian came to power in A.D. 117. The empire was so large that Hadrian thought it was smarter to protect the existing borders rather than to continue trying to expand them.

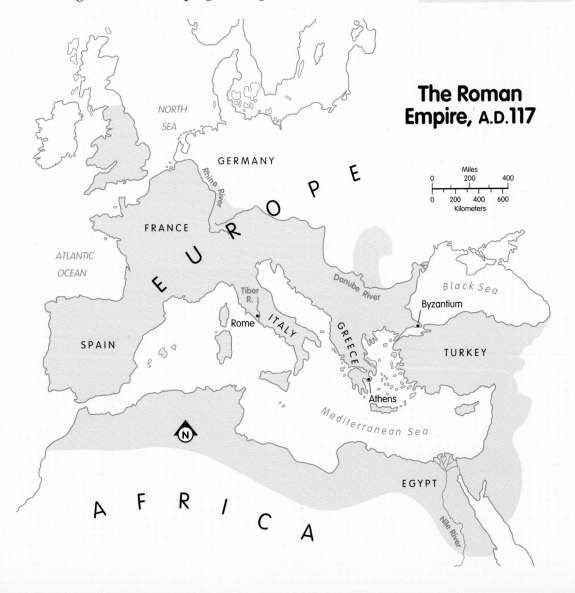

The Roman Empire, A.D.117

the laws. He even had a huge wall built along England's northern border to keep out invaders. The wall was later named Hadrian's Wall, and parts of it still stand.

Many people were angry with Hadrian's decision. They wanted the glory of winning battles and gaining more power. Also, some people thought that Hadrian's adoption had been faked, and that Hadrian was not the rightful heir to the empire. Perhaps because of these resentments, four senators even tried to kill Hadrian. When the senators' plot was discovered, they were put to death. Many people were angry, since the men had been senators for a long time and were much beloved in Rome. Hadrian claimed he had not ordered the executions, but the public still blamed him.

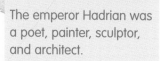

The emperor Hadrian was a poet, painter, sculptor, and architect.

These problems—occurring right at the beginning of his reign—made Hadrian unpopular and put extra pressure on him to find ways to please the people of Rome. After all, Rome was the capital city of the empire, and its citizens considered themselves the most privileged citizens in the world. Emperors needed to pay close attention to them. If the Roman people and Senate didn't like the things Hadrian did, they might try again to kill him. To gain favor, Hadrian quickly ordered that everyone in the city of Rome receive three pieces of gold—a personal gift from the new emperor.

He also launched a massive building program, erecting structures all over the Roman Empire, but especially in Rome. The building program would continue

THE END OF EXPANSION

Some important people were upset about Hadrian's end of expansion. Some, like the great orator, politician, and historian Cornelius Tacitus, complained about the lack of glory to be found in a peaceful empire. In his book *Annals*, Tacitus grumbled, "No one should compare my *Annals* with the writings of those who covered the ancient deeds of the Roman people: they could record great wars, cities besieged, kings defeated or captured . . . we must labor in a confined space, with no glory."

throughout his reign, and the ongoing construction and beautification of Rome would be a constant reminder of Hadrian's generosity and concern for the city, even when he was away traveling. All the construction would also provide work for thousands of laborers and craftspeople. People who supplied building materials would prosper as well.

Hadrian's motivation for erecting grand structures was not only popularity. More than just a soldier, he was also a poet, a painter, a sculptor, and an architect. Architecture was his particular passion. A massive building program would please the citizens, and it would also please him.

So the man who returned to Rome to find an old temple burned had imagination as well as wealth and power. The Pantheon would be a building such as no human had ever seen. Its massive dome would umbrella over its visitors just as Roman civilization umbrellaed over all Roman citizens. The perfectly rounded dome would reflect the perfection of the ideal Roman Empire: no beginning, no end, no seams or cracks or corners. And the glory of the building would reflect upon Hadrian himself. Seated under the heavenly dome, he would be the son of a god, surrounded by the heavens.

Chapter Two
PLANNING THE TEMPLE AND CLEARING THE LAND

A.D. 118

Above: Hadrian was a talented artist, but he was not a professional architect.
Opposite: Romans cutting down trees to clear space for construction

MOST ROMAN EMPERORS were not architects. They hired architects to design and construct buildings for them. Hadrian, though, was different from his predecessors. Even as a young man, he had been interested in architecture. He loved to sketch designs for buildings. He was proud of his sketches and often showed them to other people, including Trajan's architects. As he grew older, his interest in architecture remained strong. He may have insisted on being involved in the design process of every building he constructed. No one knows for sure, but the Pantheon was probably no exception.

But Hadrian was not a professional architect. He probably suggested the basic idea for the Pantheon and produced some drawings. He would not have overseen the construction of the Pantheon. A professional architect, or a team of architects, would have done that.

Some Roman emperors had a chief architect who was responsible for designing whatever the emperor wanted and seeing that it was properly built. The chief architect was in charge. All other architects on a project worked for him. Trajan's chief architect was a highly respected citizen named Apollodoros.

No one knows who Hadrian's chief architect was. Hadrian and Apollodoros knew each other, but historians don't believe Apollodoros was Hadrian's chief architect. According to Dio Cassius, a senator and historian who lived about one hundred years after Hadrian and Apollodoros, the two men did not get along.

Dio wrote that Hadrian had been humiliated by Apollodoros's criticisms of his designs. Dio reports that Hadrian was extremely ambitious to excel at every art and science and did not take Apollodoros's criticism well. He tells one story in which Hadrian, as a young man, interrupted the famous architect to show off some drawings he'd been working on. Apollodoros belittled him, saying, "Be off, and draw your pumpkins [domes]. You don't understand any of these matters."

Dio goes on to say that after Hadrian became emperor, he consulted Apollodoros on some architectural matters. Apollodoros was still

dismissive of Hadrian's ideas. Hadrian flew into a rage, first banishing Appollodoros and then having him put to death.

Dio seems to have gone out of his way in his book to portray Hadrian as jealous and bitter. Many historians suspect Dio's unflattering stories about Hadrian are exaggerations.

As for who was Hadrian's chief architect, it is most likely that Hadrian had a team of architects, master builders, and military engineers. These people probably worked together to solve the engineering problems involved in building the Pantheon. They took Hadrian's idea and turned it into a real structure. They planned every detail of the building.

CONCRETE AND ROMAN ARCHITECTURE

Before the Romans, grand public architecture was based on the Greek post-and-lintel tradition—columns holding up horizontal structures called entablatures. Erecting post-and-lintel buildings took a lot of time and skilled workers, because the pieces in the building were cut from stone and then fit together like a giant puzzle.

In the early years of the Roman Empire, the Romans invented an incredibly useful material that could

This Greek temple was built in the post-and-lintel tradition. Vertical columns hold up a horizontal entablature.

ROMAN CONCRETE

No one knows exactly what ingredients (and their exact amounts) the Romans used to make concrete. The ingredients in concrete can vary in many ways. But present-day architects would like to know because ancient Roman structures have been standing for more than two thousand years. Few modern concrete buildings will achieve such permanence. What makes Roman concrete so durable?

Scientists have discovered that a combination of lime and ash appears to be a key ingredient in Roman concrete. When lime and a special volcanic ash called pozzolana are mixed together, they create a chemical reaction which, in turn, creates an extremely hard product. So this is part of the answer. Even knowing this, though, scientists have been unable to duplicate ancient Roman concrete precisely.

largely replicate stone: concrete. The same type of concrete is found in modern sidewalks and swimming pools. The concrete used in the Pantheon was created by mixing sand, lime (a mineral obtained from limestone), ash called pozzolana from nearby volcanoes, and aggregate (rocks and chunks of brick of various sizes) with water. It could be made quickly and with little skill. It also dried quickly. And the finished product was almost as hard as stone.

Even more important than its ease of use was the fact that concrete assumed the shape of whatever mold it was poured into. The Romans learned how to construct molds from wood, tile, and bricks. Each mold produced solid structures of concrete.

Because of this new invention, the Romans were able to develop a new architectural style. With concrete, Roman architects let their imaginations run free. They built more complex buildings than any civilization before them had built, structures that could hold thousands of people. And they built more *kinds* of structures. While previous civilizations had built buildings such as houses, temples, palaces, and tombs, the Romans, with their inventions, were able to construct enormous public projects such as basilicas, aqueducts, public baths, and gigantic outdoor arenas.

Many Roman buildings featured plenty of vaults. A vault is a curved

The weight of the flat ceiling pushes straight down into the columns.

The weight of the vaulted ceiling rests in the walls, so no columns are needed to hold up the middle of the ceiling.

Right: The weight of the domed ceiling rests in the circular wall, allowing the entire ceiling to stand without any support in the middle. *Far Right:* The dome also creates hoop stress—weight pushing outward. The circular wall has to be thick and strong to support hoop stress.

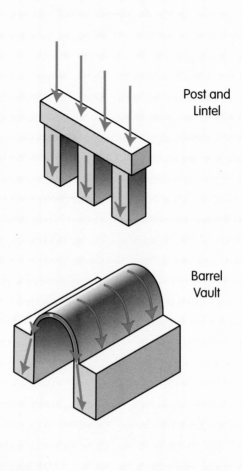

Post and Lintel

Barrel Vault

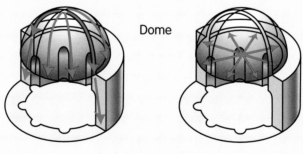

Dome

ceiling. The weight of a curved ceiling is transferred to the outer walls of a structure so it doesn't fall down. In contrast, the weight of a flat ceiling is evenly distributed among its outer walls, with a lot of weight resting in the middle of the ceiling. So a very large flat ceiling has to be supported in the middle with columns or weight-bearing walls. A vaulted ceiling, even a large one, can stand up without support in the middle. Tunnel ceilings and domes are two kinds of vaults.

Roman architects also featured plenty of arches. An arch is curved, like a vault, but shallow, like a doorway. An arched doorway holds the weight of a wall in its haunches, or sides.

Some pre-Roman buildings had arches or vaults constructed from stone blocks that were fitted together. But carving stone blocks and piecing them together was hard, tedious work that required highly skilled stonecutters. The Romans, however, could pour concrete into arch- or vault-shaped molds. They did not invent arches or vaults, but because of concrete they were able to perfect them and use them more widely.

Construction was efficient and organized. Concrete was one reason the Romans could build so efficiently. Building planners could direct hundreds of men to a building site and divide them into specialized crews: one crew to measure the ingredients for concrete, one to mix them, one to

This hot room—part of a bath building in Pompeii, Italy—has a vaulted ceiling.

construct molds, one to pour, and so on. Huge buildings with amazing vaults and arches went up in only a few years because different crews could work on different parts of a building at the same time. When using concrete, fewer skilled workers were needed to construct a building.

THE PLAN

The only remaining plans we have for the Pantheon's design are some templates inscribed in the pavement in front of the Mausoleum (tomb) of Augustus. The templates were used as a pattern for assembling part of the front of the Pantheon's porch. But other than these templates, no plans or blueprints for the Pantheon have survived. Most of what we know about how the Pantheon was built we have learned from studying the building itself. For example, we know that when Hadrian or his architects designed the Pantheon, they used a mix of older, traditional architecture, which was heavily influenced by Greek temples, and contemporary Roman architecture.

The building was designed in three parts. The first—the main portion of the building—was the rotunda, an enormous brick-and-concrete cylinder with a dome. The second—the entrance—was a more traditional porch with columns. The third was a rectangular concrete block connecting the porch to the domed cylinder.

The traditional porch was something every Roman would have been familiar with, but when combined with the huge rotunda it created a totally new form. People would approach the building by crossing a large courtyard, called a forecourt, flanked by marble columns on either side. At the far end, they would see the traditional porch with its carved stone columns. But they wouldn't have a very good view of the rotunda behind the porch. From the forecourt, the dome looked large but not especially radical. It looked like a giant saucepan with a lid on top.

Once they reached the far end of the forecourt, they would mount five steep steps and enter the porch. From there they'd move through the connecting block, walk through giant doors, and find themselves inside the rotunda.

The more normal-looking outside of the building would not prepare visitors for the awesome sight they would find inside the rotunda—a perfect hemisphere, 142 feet (43 m) in diameter, curving upward from the top of a giant round wall.

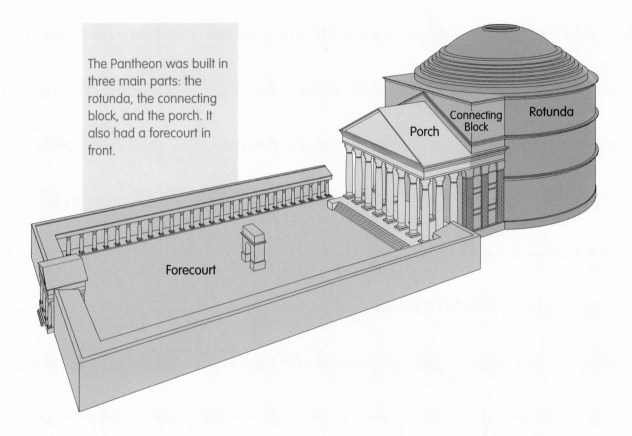

The Pantheon was built in three main parts: the rotunda, the connecting block, and the porch. It also had a forecourt in front.

Rotunda

Connecting Block

Porch

Forecourt

CLEARING THE LAND

Hadrian's Pantheon was to be located on the site of the old Pantheon, right in the middle of the Campus Martius. Once Hadrian and his architects had their plan, the first tasks were to clear the area of all the debris from the burned Pantheon and to level the ground. To build the new Pantheon and its forecourt, an area roughly the size of two football fields would have to be cleared—which was a lot of work.

For any building project in Rome, the imperial public works commission organized the labor and materials that would be needed. The commission was an administrative branch of government that primarily employed clerks, secretaries, architects, and engineers. For the Pantheon, building materials were ordered from all over the empire and transported to Rome, and the workers needed to work with them were hired. Many different kinds of workers were necessary to build the Pantheon, including stonecutters, brick masons, iron and bronze workers, sculptors, jewelers, and laborers. Many of the workers were slaves.

No one knows for sure when work on the Pantheon site started, but it must have started sometime after A.D. 118, since Hadrian wasn't in Rome until then. But once it started, it moved quickly. The workers assigned to clear the area had no electricity or gas-powered machines, like bulldozers or dump trucks. They did have ingenious machines and devices such as pulleys and cranes powered by humans or animals. Hundreds of men swarmed into the area. They raked and shoveled and hauled the charred debris. The Mediterranean sun beat down on them as they stacked the remains of the old Pantheon into donkey carts. All salvageable materials were set aside to be reused in the new Pantheon. For weeks, a dusty procession of carts carried the unusable debris to the outskirts of the city and dumped it.

A relief from the tomb of an ancient Roman family shows slaves clambering in a giant wheel *(lower left)* to provide power to operate ropes and pulleys and lift a builder's crane.

The ground was cleared and leveled in a few months. Next, building supplies had to be shipped in from all over the empire. For instance, the Pantheon's porch would have sixteen granite columns, each one 40 feet (12 m) tall and 5 feet (1.5 m) in diameter. The granite for these columns was quarried in the mountains of eastern Egypt and carved into perfect columns by skilled stonecutters. They wouldn't be needed until much later, but stonecutting was a highly skilled job that required a lot of time. The columns were chiseled at the quarries so they were lighter for their transportation to Rome. They were then dragged on wooden carts to the Nile River and floated by barge to Alexandria, where they were loaded onto ships.

After crossing the Mediterranean Sea to Italy, the enormous columns were taken off the ships, loaded onto barges, and floated up the Tiber River to Rome, where they were put on wooden carts again and hauled to the building site.

Sand was gathered from beaches throughout the Mediterranean, lime was produced from limestone, and huge loads of various rock were collected—all ingredients for concrete. Brickmakers molded, stamped, and baked tons of clay into thousands of bricks and shipped them to Rome. Supervisors coordinated the movement and receipt of all these supplies, every step of the way.

Hundreds of workers would be at the site every day, and they would have to be fed. Special teams of cooks and kitchen workers were hired to make sure that everyone had plenty of food and water. Likewise, doctors were probably stationed at the site to treat any injuries that occurred.

Preparations for finishing touches also began early. Much of this work took place off the site. Sculptors created statues. Ironmongers made clamps, bronze tiles, and metal decorations. Jewelers applied gilt to decorations. Although these people rarely came to the building site, they were still an integral part of the Pantheon's workforce.

INTO THE FUTURE... WITH THE ROMANS

The Romans had a genius for organizing and inventing things. They borrowed many ideas from other cultures and added their own improvements. Besides concrete, many Roman ideas and inventions are still with us.

- The Calendar. We still use a Roman calendar. Most of the months are named after Roman gods or emperors. March is named after the god Mars, and August is named after the emperor Augustus. The Romans also may have originated the seven-day week that we still use.

- The names of the Planets. The Romans named the planets Jupiter, Saturn, Venus, Mars, and Mercury, after Roman deities.

- Familiar Architecture. Many of the world's public buildings (libraries, town halls, and museums) are based on the designs and construction methods found in Roman architecture. Many churches are based on a Roman form called the basilica, and modern stadiums are descendants of the Roman amphitheater. The Romans were also the first to develop indoor plumbing and heating systems.

Chapter Three
THE FOUNDATION AND ROTUNDA WALLS

A.D. 118–120

As crews finished hauling away debris from the old Pantheon, crowds must have gathered at the site to see what was happening. For nearly ten years, the blackened remains of the old Pantheon had littered the Campus Martius. But with the arrival of the newly crowned emperor Hadrian and the flurry of activity at the building site, it was an exciting time for Rome. What was the new emperor going to build?

With the ground finally cleared, Hadrian's architects marked off the measurements for the building. Measuring a circular building was a lot easier than measuring a square one. The architects simply pounded a wooden stake into

The Tiber was an important river in Rome. It supplied water for the city and was used to transport people and cargo.

the ground at the center of the site. Someone stretched out a length of rope attached to the stake and walked around the stake in a circle. He marked two foundation lines as he went, one outside and one inside the ring-shaped foundation. For a squared-off building, an architect would have had to engineer the corner angles exactly right, or the whole building would have been crooked.

Because the Pantheon's site was so close to the Tiber River, the ground was slightly swampy. Sometimes the river flooded. Hadrian's architects knew they had to build a strong foundation to prevent the building from sinking into the mud. Building a solid foundation was also crucial because the Pantheon's dome would weigh more than 5,000 tons (4,535 metric tons)—more than the weight of four thousand full-grown elephants. The rotunda walls would weigh even more. In any type of architecture, the foundation is the most important part of the structure. The foundation supports all the weight of the finished building and enables the building to stand up. The Pantheon's foundation would also raise the Pantheon slightly above the flooding level.

The first step was to dig a ring-shaped trench between the two foundation lines. The trench was about 15 feet (4.5 m) deep. At the bottom

of the trench the workers reached river clay that was bluish in color. They built a circular brick wall around the outside wall of the trench and filled the hole with concrete. After the trench was filled, it had become the foundation that would anchor the Pantheon in the ground. At the top of the foundation, the workers filled in the center of the circle with concrete to create a giant concrete pad. The top of the foundation would be the Pantheon's floor.

THE ROTUNDA WALL

After the foundation had set, it was time to build the 20-foot-thick (6-m-thick) circular wall of the rotunda. Each day workers arrived at the site and broke into teams. A constant stream of wagons rumbled into the area, loaded with supplies. Some teams did nothing but unload supplies. Bricks had to be stacked in different areas of the site, where bricklayers could reach them easily. Sand, lime, pozzolana, and aggregate had to be shoveled from carts and put in piles. Wood for molds and scaffolding had to be stacked at the site. Every day more supplies arrived and had to be unloaded. Materials were carried in baskets because the Romans did not have wheelbarrows. Some workers measured ingredients for making concrete. They placed all the ingredients in huge buckets, and then other workers added water and mixed the concrete.

The rotunda wall can be thought of as two circular brick walls, one placed inside the other, with a core of concrete sandwiched between them. The first, interior brick wall is 142 feet (43 m) in diameter, the same diameter as the interior of the building. The second circular brick wall was built 20 feet (6 m) out from the first wall.

Teams of workers hauled bricks, mixed mortar, and built up the walls brick by brick. They laid the bricks in courses, or sections, that were about 2 feet (0.6 m) high. The space between the inner and outer walls was then filled with concrete, one section at a time. Each section was probably about one day's worth of work.

To make anything out of concrete—a vault, an arch, a wall—a mold has to be constructed. A mold is a frame, or shell, that holds a liquid. When concrete is first mixed, it is wet and sloppy. Without a mold, it would ooze and then harden into a shapeless mass. The rotunda wall's mold was the two circular brick walls. Concrete was poured between the two brick walls, becoming one huge, thick wall in the process. The

The concrete used in modern construction is basically the same as the concrete used by the ancient Romans.

brick walls remained in place and became part of the finished structure, like an inner and outer skin.

As the brick walls went higher and concrete was poured between them, an enormous cylindrical drum began to take shape. This is the rotunda wall.

As soon as the Pantheon walls were higher than workers could reach, they had to find ways to keep going higher. Ladders weren't effective for large buildings. They couldn't reach high enough, nor could they hold more than one person. So carpenters had to construct scaffolds.

A scaffold is a temporary framework that attaches to a building. As a building goes up, workers use ladders to reach the platforms in the scaffolding. Then they stand on the scaffolding as they continue working.

To be safe, scaffolds have to be anchored to a building. During Roman times, logs called putlogs anchored a scaffold to a building. The end of a log was placed in a hole in the wall and cemented in place. The scaffold was then attached to the log. When the construction had gone as high as the scaffold allowed, another level of scaffolding was added, and the process was repeated, higher up the wall. Whenever a log was removed, a hole remained where it used to be. These holes are called putlog holes and are still visible on the Pantheon.

BAYS AND STONEWORK IN THE DRUM

The drum is not an uninterrupted circle. Many voids, or empty pockets, were carefully built into it. The brick skin was built around the shape of these voids. On the inside of the drum the Pantheon's architects built eight large niches, or bays, into the wall. One of these openings went all

Each of the bays built into the rotunda wall have two tall columns in front.

the way through the wall and became the building's entrance. The other seven bays were so deep they reached more than halfway to the back (or outside) of the rotunda wall. The bays were more than tall enough for a person to walk around inside, but they probably held statues. Besides being decoration, the bays served a functional purpose. Because they were large areas where no concrete had been poured, they lightened the weight of the rotunda and the load on the foundation was lessened.

Stonework decorated the inside of the rotunda. Two elaborately carved marble columns were built in at the front of each bay. Above the bays, two marble cornices were installed. A cornice is a lip, or horizontal molding, that is embedded in a wall and projects outward for decoration. The cornices circled the inside of the rotunda, one halfway up the wall and one at the top of the wall.

Because this stone decoration was built into the walls, it had to be installed while the walls were being built. But some of the Pantheon's decorations were installed after construction was complete.

CHAMBERS AND ARCHES IN THE DRUM

The architects also built voids into the outside of the rotunda wall. From the outside of the building, square openings and brick arches are visible at different levels. The square openings lead to open chambers. The arcs that appear to be arches are actually the ends of powerful vaults that help distribute the weight of the drum over these chambers and over the bays on the inside. The vaults radiate all the way through the drum, from the inside to the outside. They provide an important system for supporting the dome. Together with the open chambers, the vaults also reduce the weight of the rotunda wall by 25 percent.

The mold for a concrete vault was a wooden vault. Concrete was poured over the wooden vault. When it hardened, the wooden vault was removed and the concrete vault remained in place. In some Roman buildings, including the Pantheon, marks are still visible in the hardened concrete where the wood used to be. Most of the vaults in the

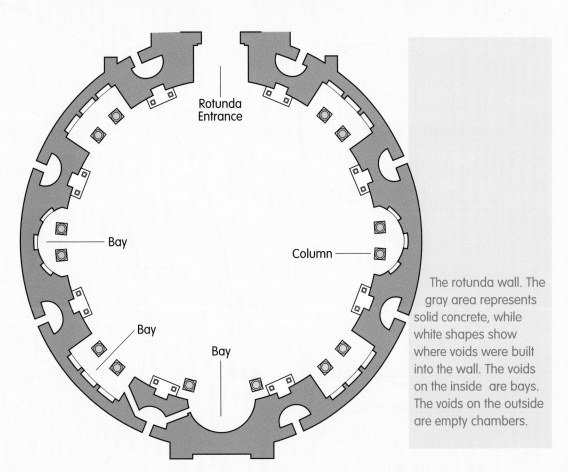

Rotunda
Entrance

Bay

Column

Bay

Bay

The rotunda wall. The gray area represents solid concrete, while white shapes show where voids were built into the wall. The voids on the inside are bays. The voids on the outside are empty chambers.

Square openings visible on the outside of the rotunda lead to empty chambers. Brick arches—actually the ends of powerful vaults—are visible above the openings

rotunda walls are lined with bricks or tiles. The bricks or tiles were laid over the wooden vault and covered with concrete. They remained in the wall after the concrete had hardened and the wooden vault had been removed.

EXCITEMENT IN ROME

With so many workers doing so many tasks at once, the noise at the Pantheon site was deafening. Clouds of dust filled the air, and the pounding of hammers rang through the streets of Rome. Teams of carpenters built wooden scaffolds alongside the walls so that workers could climb up and keep working as the walls went higher and higher. More skilled carpenters hammered out wooden molds for arches and vaults. No one could have been unaware of the work that was going on.

By responding to his critics with generosity, Hadrian may have made himself more popular than he had been when he first became emperor. Besides putting up buildings, he also forgave the debts of all people who owed money to the government. In a public show of generosity, he burned all the debt papers in a giant bonfire. The people were extremely grateful. They even built a monument in the place where the ceremonial burning

THE GRUNT WORK

Gangs of slaves or free laborers (*below*) who had few skills usually did the hardest physical labor in Roman construction projects. Tasks such as hauling and stacking bricks, shoveling sand, and sorting aggregate by size and weight were usually performed by these workers.

People from most social backgrounds could have worked on crews that handled more skilled jobs, such as the construction of wooden molds or brick walls. Anyone who was talented at a given skill could be moved up to a higher position. Even a slave, if he was talented, was likely to be freed in order to pursue a career in his trade.

had taken place. On the base of the monument was carved a legend that said Hadrian had "provided security not merely for his present citizens but also for their descendants by this generosity." Not long afterward, coins were minted that celebrated the act again. Soon, Hadrian left Rome to visit provinces in southern Italy.

Chapter Four
A HEAVENLY DOME

A.D. 120–125

WHEN THE GREAT DRUM OF the Pantheon was finished, around A.D. 120, it was time to start construction on the dome. Supply wagons still rumbled onto the site, just as they had during earlier parts of the project. Workers still measured out portions of sand, aggregate, pozzolana, and lime. Carpenters still hammered scaffolding together. And foremen still strode about the site, shouting out instructions. But at this point, teams of master carpenters became the focus of the operation.

Brick walls worked well to mold the concrete in the drum. But bricks were too heavy to serve as a mold for the concrete dome. Instead, the dome's mold was constructed out of wood by these highly skilled carpenters. The mold was probably propped on top of the drum's upper cornice using flying centering. Flying centering was a complicated network of supporting timber beams that rested on the lip of the drum and reached over the entire dome. The timber beams for the flying centering had to be strong. And the construction had to be sturdy in order to support the weight of the mold and the concrete that would eventually be poured over it. Cranes, perched on the drum at the level of the cornice and manipulated by ropes from the ground, were used to lift the huge timber beams up to the cornice.

The construction of the mold itself was espe-

Above: A view of the interior of the Pantheon's dome.
Opposite: Flying centering was probably propped on the upper interior cornice and may have looked like this.

cially difficult because the interior of the dome was going to be covered with an intricate waffle-shaped pattern of indentations called coffers. The coffers had to be placed on the exterior of the wooden dome mold so that they would later be imprinted into the concrete as it was poured. The pattern of coffers was so intricate that the coffer molds could only be built by master carpenters. The work the master

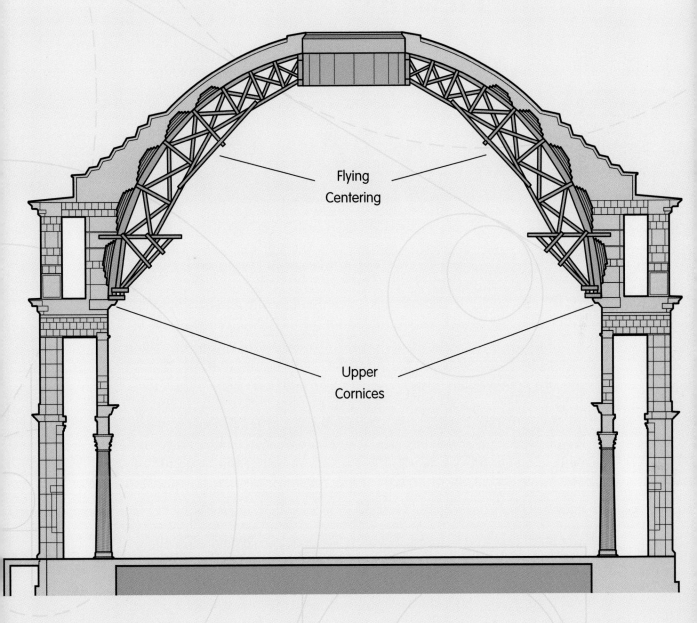

Flying
Centering

Upper
Cornices

A fresco, or wall painting, from the first century A.D., showing Roman construction workers

carpenters did was far more difficult and complex than that of any worker who mixed and poured concrete.

The entire wooden mold for the dome was probably constructed on top of the flying centering all at once. But the coffer molds were installed and the concrete was poured in sections. There are five rings of coffers on the interior of the dome, each ring smaller than the one beneath it. Workers assembled each ring of coffer molds separately. Like busy ants, they climbed up scaffolds and put the coffer molds in place against the dome mold. When a whole ring of coffer molds was in place, they poured concrete over that ring. While the concrete hardened, the workers prepared the next ring of coffer molds.

Nearly all work on the Pantheon was hazardous, but work on the dome was particularly dangerous. The dome could be worked on only from scaffolds. And scaffolds—even modern-day scaffolds—aren't very sturdy. As the dome went higher, workers found themselves hauling large wooden coffer molds and heavy buckets of concrete onto rickety wooden platforms high above the ground. Even the lowest section of the dome is more than 70 feet (21 m) off the ground. A fall from that height would have killed or seriously injured a worker.

While all this work was being done, measures had to be taken to protect the fine stonework inside the drum. The cornices and columns had been painstakingly carved. No one wanted to see them damaged by falling tools or wooden beams. Much of this stonework was probably encased in wood to protect it.

KEEPING THE DOME IN THE AIR

Hadrian's architects used several techniques to make sure that the enormous dome would stay up. One technique was the coffers. The pattern of coffers is interesting to look at, but the coffers are more than just decoration. Each coffer reduces the weight of the dome.

EARLY DOMES

The Romans began experimenting with domes at least as early as 100 B.C. Concrete had been invented at least half a century earlier, and Roman architects gradually developed a mastery of this new building material.

One of the best-preserved early domes was constructed at Baiae, a resort town on the Bay of Naples in southern Italy, more than one hundred years before Hadrian's reign. It was part of a large warm-bath complex. This dome had a diameter of approximately 74 feet (22.5 m). Like the Pantheon, it had an oculus, or circular opening, at the top.

When the concrete hardened and the coffer molds were removed, they left empty spaces where they had been. Recent engineering studies have shown that the coffers only remove about 5 percent of the total weight of the dome. But 5 percent of a dome that weighs 5,000 tons (4,535 metric tons) is a lot—250 tons (227 metric tons), or 500,000 pounds (227,000 kilograms).

The Pantheon's architects also had a strong understanding of various construction materials, especially concrete. They figured out that by changing the aggregate (the chunks of rock or brick in concrete), they could change the weight of the concrete. As the dome of the Pantheon rises, each level is lighter than the one beneath it because the architect changed the aggregate in each level.

The lower levels contain the heaviest aggregate. Chunks of basalt and travertine, both very hard and strong, make up most of the drum's concrete. Higher up the drum, tufa (porous volcanic rock) is mixed in. Above the drum, the lower rings of the dome contain brick fragments. At the uppermost level of the dome, the aggregate is tiny pieces of pumice. Pumice is a type of aerated volcanic rock that is lightweight but strong.

Because of the dome's shape, its weight naturally pushes outward as well as downward. The weight pushing outward is called hoop stress. Hoop stress complicates the problem of keeping the dome from crumbling. The architects counteracted the hoop stress by starting the inward slope of the bottom of the dome inside the rotunda wall. The outside of the rotunda wall is higher than the inside. From the outside, people can't tell where the bottom of the dome is, because it starts inside the rotunda wall. The higher outside wall acts as shoulders for the dome, holding it in.

The architects also manipulated the thickness of the dome. They made the bottom thicker than the

This color-coded illustration shows how the density of the concrete used in the Pantheon changes. The densest (and strongest) concrete is in the foundation and floor. The concrete above that, in the lowest section of the rotunda wall, is slightly less dense, and the level above that is even less dense. The highest part of the building, near the oculus, has the least dense concrete of all.

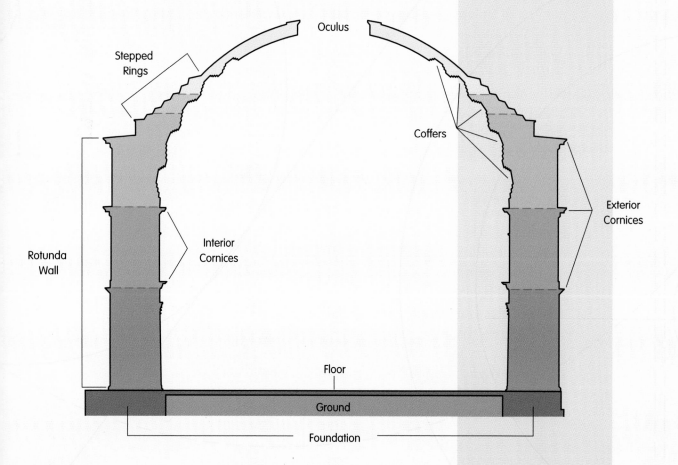

THE STEPPED RINGS

It is traditionally believed that the stepped rings act as buttresses for the dome. But some scholars argue that the stepped rings don't actually support the dome. Some argue that the rings were not built for any structural reasons, but simply because they made construction easier. The bottom of the dome is the steepest part, and it may have been very difficult to apply concrete there. The stepped rings would have served as flat terraces to hold the concrete.

top. To do this, they built several stepped rings at the bottom of the outside of the dome. By adding weight to the outside edge of the dome, the stepped rings act as buttresses, or supports. The weight of the stepped rings pushes downward into the thick drum, which helps counteract the tendency of the dome to push outward. At the ring level, the dome is nearly as thick as the drum. But as the dome rises, it becomes thinner. At the top of the dome, the concrete is only 5 to 6 feet (1.5 to 1.8 m) thick, making the top of the dome by far the lightest part of the structure.

No other construction material, such as stone, brick, wood, or metal, could have allowed the architects the freedom to build the dome as creatively as concrete did. Concrete is heavy. But its flexibility allowed the Pantheon's architects to make the dome light.

THE OCULUS

The part of the dome that weighs least of all is the very center, at the top: it weighs nothing. That's because the Pantheon's dome was never closed at the top. Instead, the architects left a round opening nearly 30 feet (9 m) across. Called an oculus ("eye," in Latin), this opening was reinforced with a row of bricks. The oculus allows sunlight to enter the Pantheon, providing the only source of light inside. There are no windows in the rotunda, and few electric lights have been installed.

The oculus is regarded as the most spectacular feature of the Pantheon, because the light it provides brings the rotunda to life. Although the area of the oculus is small compared to the area inside the rotunda, the light it provides is dramatic. The sun shines through the oculus and beams a bright shaft of light into the rotunda. As the sun moves across the sky over the course of a day, the light in the rotunda moves too. A glowing circle slides across the walls and floor, and shadows in the coffers and bays are constantly shifting.

The oculus also allows rain to fall into the Pantheon. This meant that drains had to be installed in the floor of the Pantheon. Otherwise the building would have turned into a swimming pool the first time it rained.

When the dome was completed, around A.D. 125 or earlier, workers pulled away the flying centering and wooden dome mold. This work, called decentering, exposed the finished concrete dome. The Pantheon's oculus was probably very important in protecting the marble columns and cornices during decentering. The timber beams were probably tied to ropes suspended from the oculus and swung harmlessly to the center of the building before being lowered to the floor.

Afterward, wooden boards, piles of sand, and broken tools littered the site, inside and out. Different sections of concrete were different shades of muddy gray. Before the concrete was completely set, large, discolored patches splotched the walls. Romans didn't have much of a view of the building anyway, because all the scaffolds were still in place. Workers needed to crawl over the building, putting all the ornamentation in place. They also had to build the porch and connecting block. The biggest part of construction was finished, but the Pantheon was not.

The Pantheon's dome is a perfect hemisphere. If it were expanded into a full sphere, it would fit perfectly inside the rotunda.

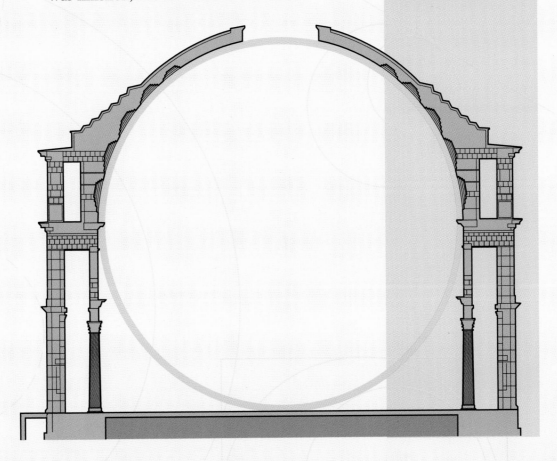

Chapter Five

THE TEMPLE TAKES SHAPE

A.D. 125–128

WORK ON THE CONNECTING block and porch probably came last, beginning about when the dome was being decentered. If they had been built earlier, they would have been in the way during construction of the rotunda. The cranes that lifted the timber beams inside the rotunda required people to pull on ropes from outside the building. The pulling took place in the cleared area all around the rotunda.

A cutaway drawing of the Pantheon shows the connecting block and porch extending off the front of the rotunda.

The connecting block, like the rotunda, was built mainly of concrete. It is about as tall as the upper exterior cornice of the rotunda. Like the rotunda, it has vaulted chambers in its upper stories. It also has two staircases leading to the roof. In the front of the block are two bays, where statues of Augustus (the first Roman emperor) and Agrippa (the builder of the original Pantheon) are believed to have stood.

The workers built the porch on the front of the block. The porch was built in the traditional, Greek style of architecture—columns holding up an entablature. There are sixteen marble-and-granite columns in the porch.

Above the porch's entablature rests a pediment (a triangular-shaped top), which faces the front of the building. To make sure the pieces of the pediment fit together, the workers assembled them on the ground on top of a template in front of the Mausoleum of Augustus, north of the Pantheon on the Campus Martius. They used cranes to raise the massive columns and move them into place and then to lift the pediment on top of them.

The Pantheon. The traditional porch with rows of columns makes for an impressive entrance.

The top of the pediment is about half as high as the top of the dome.

The porch sat on a raised platform and had five marble steps leading up to it. It is about two-thirds as wide as the rotunda. Eight columns line the front of the porch at the top of the steps, and the other eight are arranged behind them, creating three aisles. The center aisle is the widest and leads into the connecting block and then to a pair of huge bronze doors. The doors are the entrance to the rotunda. Each of the narrower aisles beside the center aisle leads to one of the bays on the front of the connecting block.

Historians argue about the porch. Its design is so different from the main portion of the Pantheon, some argue that the architect simply ran out of ideas and attached a porch to the building so people could enter the dome. Others think Hadrian attached a

A Bigger Porch?

One scholar argues that the Pantheon's porch was supposed to be 25 percent bigger, which would have been more balanced with the size of the rotunda. But the architect had to change his plans when the one-piece 50-foot (15-m) granite columns he wanted could not be quarried on schedule. Only 40-foot (12-m) columns could be pulled from the granite quarry in Egypt.

The architect would have had a few ways he could deal with his problem. He could have waited for as long as it took to produce the 50-footers. But emperors did not like to wait, so that option was probably not very appealing to the architect. He could have pieced together smaller hunks of granite to create 50-foot columns. But he preferred to use monolithic columns. Monolithic columns are columns made from one piece of stone. Monolithic columns are stronger than columns assembled from more than one piece and could be put up much quicker. He also could have used another kind of rock, like marble. But granite is stronger than marble. Also, the kind of granite that Hadrian wanted was rare and hard to quarry. That made it more prestigious. Hadrian may have insisted on this kind of rare granite for the Pantheon.

The only choice the architect would have had left was to use the 40-footers. But shorter columns meant making the entire porch smaller.

traditional porch as a way of softening the radical aspect of the dome, which was such a break from traditional architecture.

DECORATING THE PANTHEON

The Pantheon was built for the effect of its interior space, but the outside of the building was made beautiful too. The porch and connecting block were covered with veneers, or thin sheets, of marble or travertine limestone. Workers hefted and hauled the sheets of stone up the scaffolds and attached them to the side of the building with iron clamps. The outside of the Pantheon's rotunda wall was covered with stucco.

Bronze and other kinds of metal were used extensively in the building of the Pantheon. Bronze is a metal that is made by mixing copper and tin together. The exterior of the dome was covered with gilded bronze tiles. In sunlight, the Pantheon glowed a brilliant gold. The extra weight of these bronze tiles was something the architect had to account for when designing the dome. Besides the roof tiles, bronze was used to encase wooden beams used in the porch roof, and a bronze ceiling was also placed in the porch. Metal clamps were used to attach marble veneers and other decoration and to hold all stone blocks and columns in place.

Most of the decoration was applied inside the rotunda. The bays the workers had built most likely held statues. Each probably held a statue of a god, since the Pantheon was a temple for all the gods. Jupiter, the god of light, the sky, and the Roman state, probably held the most prominent spot—directly across from the entrance. Between each bay, a small temple-front projects from the wall. A temple-front is a shrine. Each temple-front is raised on a podium, flanked by two columns, and has a pediment on top.

A temple-front to the right of a bay. The floors and walls of the interior of the Pantheon are decorated with colored marble.

The rotunda floor was covered with huge, thin slabs of marble. The marble slabs were circles and squares laid out so that the floor looked like a giant checkerboard that was set up with circular pieces and ready to play. The marble slabs had probably been sawed and filed to shape off site, brought in on carts, and carefully lowered into place on the floor.

Above the lower cornice, the wall was decorated with a band of white marble with blue veins. Pilasters (rectangular columns) projected from the wall.

STUCCO AND GILT

Most of the Pantheon was constructed from bricks and concrete. But many other materials were used to finish it. Stucco and gilt were two of the main finishing materials.

Much of the original stucco is still visible. Stucco is made by mixing lime, sand, cement, and pigments (color) with water. It is applied to a wall, or building surface, the way plaster is applied. Stucco dries very hard, forming a protective surface.

We also know that gilt was used in the Pantheon, possibly lining the coffers or lower interior sections of the dome. Any metal can be used to make gilt, but in Roman times the most common metal used was gold. To make gilt, metal is heated until soft, then pounded or rolled into sheets that are as thin as paper. The sheets are then applied like wallpaper to a surface.

These finishing techniques were special jobs that required skilled labor. Workers who did these jobs were artisans, often coming from families of artisans. It took several years to acquire the artistic skills necessary to work on a building like the Pantheon. If a person didn't come from an artisan family, he could still become a gilt maker or other artisan. Teenaged children apprenticed with artisans by paying for the training, the way we pay to go to college. Poorer people could do an apprenticeship by doing extra work or trading things for the experience.

A goldsmith at work

Blind (false) windows were installed and were probably fitted with gilded bronze grills. Marble veneering in a pattern of circles and rectangles filled the areas between these elements. The granite and marble that made up the floor slabs, columns, cornices, temple-fronts, and pilasters was a dazzling array of colors such as yellow-orange, dark red, green-black, and blue-white. The undersides of the cornices were gilded in gold.

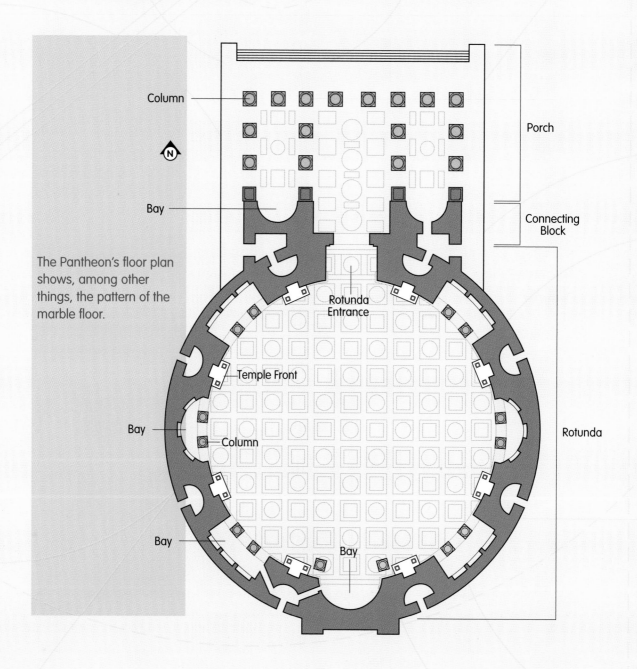

The Pantheon's floor plan shows, among other things, the pattern of the marble floor.

Column

Bay

N

Porch

Connecting Block

Rotunda Entrance

Temple Front

Bay

Column

Bay

Bay

Rotunda

Though the rotunda walls and floor were beautifully decorated, the focus of the building was the dome, and that too was decorated. The ring of the oculus was lined with gilded bronze molding. Each coffer had a sculpted rosette, or flower, in the center. Each rosette was made by a blacksmith, then gilded in bronze by a jeweler. Workers climbed up scaffolds and attached a rosette in the center of each coffer. Attaching the rosettes was dangerous work. By the time a worker got to the top row of coffering, he was roughly 110 feet (34 m) off the floor—as high as if he were standing on top of an eleven-story apartment building. Tools dropped from this height would have killed anyone they hit, such as a worker laying marble for the floor. Workers who fell from the scaffold would have been killed instantly.

THE FORECOURT

The Pantheon sat at the end of a long yard, or forecourt, that was lined by columns and had a freestanding arch in the middle. We don't know how many columns surrounded the forecourt because everything, including the arch, has disappeared with the passage of time. There may have been as many as fifty columns surrounding the forecourt, and each one of them would have been chiseled and hand-carved by master stonecutters.

The forecourt provided an impressive lead-in to the Pantheon. Romans entered the forecourt and at the other end hunched the massive temple. After crossing the forecourt, visitors entered the Pantheon through its porch.

THE PANTHEON IS FINISHED

Somewhere around 125, Hadrian returned to Rome. He had spent the last few years on imperial business in the provinces of the Roman Empire. He had made a deliberate effort to please people in the provinces, starting new building projects and passing out money wherever he went.

Work on the Pantheon wrapped up right around this time. As the Pantheon neared completion, the architects and foremen scurried about, hurrying all the workers along, shouting out orders for the clean-up. Everything had to be finished and ready for Emperor Hadrian's return. The scaffolds were dismantled from the top downward.

Bricks and Dates

The Pantheon's dedication said it was built by Agrippa. Because Hadrian kept Agrippa's original dedication, for hundreds of years people misunderstood who built the building. Even Dio Cassius, who wrote a history of Rome only one hundred years after the Pantheon's construction, wrote that the Pantheon of his own day was built by Agrippa. But the architectural design and construction techniques were too advanced for Agrippa's time period. Many people thought that Agrippa had built the porch and Hadrian had later attached the domed structure.

It wasn't until the 1900s that people figured out that the Pantheon had been built entirely by Hadrian. They figured it out by examining the bricks in the building.

During Roman times, brickmakers stamped bricks with the names of their brickyards, the names of government officials, and other datable information. By studying large numbers of ancient bricks—which can be seen in actual buildings, in ruins, and during the restoration of structures—historians have figured out who many of the major brickmakers were, and when their bricks were made.

A building couldn't have been built any earlier than the earliest dateable brick. Thus brick stamps establish a construction time for a building. Throughout most of the Pantheon, including the porch, the brick stamps are from the early 120s.

The workers yanked out the putlogs and filled or covered the putlog holes, and they hauled away all the wood. With the scaffolds down, the entire Pantheon was visible for the very first time.

What a sight it was! The Pantheon still overwhelms people with its soaring dome, which seems to defy gravity, and its magnificently illuminated space, even with little remaining ornamentation. But when it was brand new, everything was sparkling clean and glowing with gilt, colored marble, and gold and bronze. Also remarkable was the fact that this elaborate building had been constructed in less than ten years.

Although Hadrian's new, rebuilt Pantheon wasn't anything like the previous ones, he ordered the old dedication to be reproduced faithfully. He even kept the name of Marcus Agrippa, the long-dead deputy of Augustus who had built the first Pantheon for Augustus back in 27 B.C., rather than his own name. The dedication read, and still reads: "Marcus Agrippa the son of Lucius, three times consul, built this," in Latin.

This single action—dedicating the building to someone else—confused later historians for centuries. Because of the dedication, they assumed that the building had been built by Agrippa. For centuries, the true builder of the Pantheon was a mystery.

Chapter Six

THE PANTHEON AND THE ROMAN EMPIRE

A.D. 128–609

A drawing of the rotunda from its entrance shows what it may have looked like with all its decorations intact, including the statues.

HADRIAN'S NEW PANTHEON carried tremendous symbolism, much of which would have been jarring to Romans. The use of a dome in a temple was unheard of. Domed rotundas usually appeared on tombs. For Romans, temples (for worshiping gods) and tombs (for holding the dead) were never combined in the same place. The Pantheon was an obvious break with tradition. It was dedicated to the gods but called to mind tombs of the dead.

The deification of dead emperors already blurred the line between the gods and the dead. Based on what they know about Hadrian and about Roman religion during his reign, scholars believe that Hadrian's Pantheon probably celebrated the imperial cult (dead emperors as gods) as much as—or more than—it celebrated the traditional Roman gods. However, we only know of three statues that were definitely in the Pantheon (from Dio Cassius's history of Rome): Mars, the god of war; Venus, the goddess of love; and one human, Julius Caesar, the adoptive father of Augustus. Even though he was not an emperor, Julius Caesar was the first human to be deified after death by the Romans.

Even the position of the Pantheon was symbolic. The Pantheon faces almost due north and is directly aligned with the Mausoleum of Augustus. Scholars believe that Hadrian positioned the Pantheon this way to pay tribute to Augustus and also to associate himself with the great emperor. Augustus was regarded as a god, and Hadrian would have been eager to be seen in that light.

The dome itself was an important symbol: a dome, with no corners and no beginning or end, showed continuity, perfection, and permanence—just as the Roman Empire was seen as continuous, perfect, and permanent. These attributes also belonged to the heavens, the home of the Roman gods. By symbolizing both the empire and the gods, the great dome of the Pantheon linked Roman government and Roman religion. When Hadrian held court under the dome, the association would have been clear: this emperor is all powerful (just look at the building he's sitting in). He is related to the gods. And he rules an empire that is approved of and watched over by the gods.

The Pantheon was not the only place Hadrian held court and conducted imperial business. The Forum, a large open space where the

ANCIENT ROMAN RELIGION

The Pantheon was a temple, but the ancient Romans did not hold regular religious services there like people do in modern temples and churches. The priests did not give sermons. Most worship was done in private, in a person's own home.

Roman religion was very different from most religions practiced in modern times. Romans worshiped many gods, to whom they made sacrifices in exchange for the gods' goodwill. A common sacrifice was an animal. The most common animals chosen were oxen, pigs, sheep, and chickens. Male animals were offered to gods and female animals were offered to goddesses. After the animal was killed, the best meat was offered to the god. The rest was cooked and eaten by the worshiper.

Roman religion was not spiritual, like most modern religions. Instead, it was practical. If the Romans made sacrifices, they could expect the gods to take care of them. If they received good fortune, they needed to thank the appropriate god. Religion was not a personal "calling" for anyone. It was part of the government. Priests were public officers elected by the Senate. Usually priests got elected because they were prominent politicians. Roman gods were not inherently moral, and they did not ask their worshipers to live morally. They did reward faithfulness.

Jupiter was the god of light, the sky and weather, and the Roman state. He was also the king of the gods. Jupiter's wife, Juno, was the goddess of light, birth, women, and marriage. Their daughter, Minerva, was the goddess of wisdom. The three of them were the most important gods. There were other important gods. Apollo was the god of sunlight, prophecy, music, and poetry. Mars was the god of war. Vesta was the goddess of the hearth fire. Dionysus was the god of wine. And Venus was the goddess of love. The Romans also worshiped a goddess named Roma, the personification of the Roman city and state. Hadrian built a temple to Venus and Roma that still stands.

Jupiter *(left)*, the god of light, the sky and weather, and the Roman state, was the most important Roman god. Juno *(top left)*—who was the goddess of light, birth, women, and marriage— was his wife. Their daughter, Minerva *(right)*, was the goddess of wisdom.

Senate house and many courts stood, was the center of all public affairs. And there were other meeting places. Dio Cassius wrote in his history of Rome that Hadrian "transacted with the aid of the Senate all the important and urgent business and held court with the assistance of the foremost men, in the Forum or the Pantheon or various other places, always seated on a tribunal, so that whatever was done was made public."

Wherever the Senate met, it had to be a consecrated, or sacred, space. Public affairs could only be discussed in consecrated space. In this regard the Pantheon, a temple, was perfect.

THE ARCHITECT EMPEROR'S REIGN COMES TO AN END

In A.D. 130, only a few years after the opening of the Pantheon, Hadrian and his entourage were visiting Egypt. During the visit, Hadrian's best friend and companion, a young man named Antinoüs, drowned in the Nile River. The death of Antinoüs sent Hadrian into a deep depression from which he never fully recovered. For the remaining eight years of his life, Hadrian displayed little interest in government matters, and he made poor military decisions.

Hadrian returned to Rome in A.D. 134 after a six-year journey. Once back in the city, he continued to pour money into building projects in Rome and at his private estate, Tivoli. He also had become moody and suspicious of his friends and advisers. He made many enemies and is rumored to have put a lot of people to death, often unfairly. His popularity in Rome declined.

Soon Hadrian began construction on his own mausoleum. He built it on the other side of the Tiber River and connected it to the Campus Martius with a bridge. As Hadrian grew closer to death, he became increasingly bitter and sad and was in a lot of pain. But he tried to hide these feelings. He wrote in a letter to Antoninus Pius, his adopted son (and the next emperor of the Roman Empire), "I want you to know that I am being released from life neither prematurely nor unreasonably; I am not full of self-pity nor am I surprised and my faculties are unimpaired." By the time he died, in A.D. 138 at the age of 62, he was despised by the people of Rome. He was never deified. The Pantheon would be his greatest and most lasting legacy.

Although Hadrian died an unpopular man, most historians acknowledge that he had been a successful ruler. He had given the

Drawing of the
Mausoleum of Hadrian

empire firm boundaries and stable government for over twenty years. Even Dio Cassius, who had written negatively about Hadrian in his history of Rome, admitted that Hadrian was hated by the people in spite of his generally excellent rule. He said the reason people hated Hadrian was because he had unfairly put some people to death, including the four senators who had plotted against Hadrian at the beginning of his reign. Dio Cassius called them murders that were unjust.

THE FALL OF THE WEST ROMAN EMPIRE

The next few emperors after Hadrian were able to maintain the Roman Empire and protect its borders. But by 180, the Empire was in trouble. Germanic tribes were

LITTLE SOUL

Hadrian was sick—probably with some form of heart disease—for many months before he died, and he suffered great pain. He was hemorrhaging and had trouble breathing. Several times he asked his friends to kill him, but most of them feared they would be punished if they did. He also tried to kill himself. This poem, which has been translated from the original Latin by the historian Anthony Birley, was written by Hadrian during the last days of his life.

Little soul, little wanderer, little charmer,
body's guest and companion,
to what places will you set out for now?
To darkling, cold and gloomy ones—
and you won't make your usual jokes.

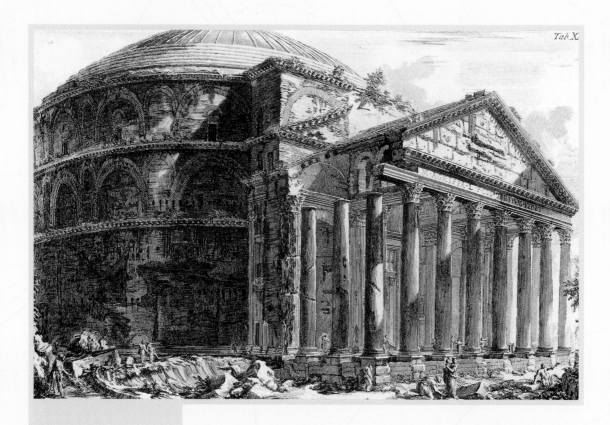

Tab.X.

This drawing shows what the Pantheon may have looked like after years without maintenance.

constantly attacking its borders. In 284 a Roman general named Diocletian was proclaimed emperor, but he quickly realized that one man could no longer govern such a large empire. He divided the empire into small units with local governments. Then he appointed a soldier named Maximian to rule the western units. Diocletian himself ruled the eastern ones.

Diocletian's reforms temporarily stabilized the Roman Empire. In 330 the emperor Constantine moved the capital from Rome to Byzantium, which he renamed Constantinople (modern Istanbul, Turkey). With the movement of the government, Roman buildings, including the Pantheon, went without maintenance. Many of them eventually became overgrown with vegetation and fell into ruin. The empire itself also began to fall into decline.

In 337 a fight among five men broke out for control of the empire, further weakening the unity of the empire. During this century, Roman religion gave way to Christianity, and the empire was permanently split into the West Roman Empire and the East Roman Empire. The East Roman Empire became known as the Byzantine Empire and continued until 1453.

The West Roman Empire—where Rome was—was conquered by a German general named Odoacer in 476. It became a patchwork of kingdoms with no centralized government. The population in Rome declined, and some water systems, roads, and buildings fell into disrepair. The city's creative activity declined as well, especially architectural creativity.

THE PANTHEON WITHOUT MAINTENANCE

As power, influence, and creativity shifted away from the city of Rome, the Pantheon deteriorated somewhat over the years. The banks of the Tiber flooded frequently, depositing mud and muck over the Campus Martius. With few government services left, the area was never cleaned out. The ground rose up around the building. Rubble left behind by fires also added to the buildup of the ground. By 600 the entrance to the Pantheon was at ground level, whereas the original visitors had had to mount five steep steps to enter.

During the same years, dirt accumulated inside the building and blocked the drains in the floor. When rain fell through the oculus, it watered the soil. Trees, shrubs, and vines began growing beneath the dome. Some historians believe that people began living inside the Pantheon, pitching tents and roasting goats over open fires.

By 600 things were looking very bleak for the Pantheon. Were it not for a pope, the Pantheon probably would not have survived, nearly intact, as it has.

Chapter Seven
STILL STANDING
A.D. 609 to
Modern Times

Pope Boniface IV *(above)* saved the Pantheon from further decline by consecrating it as a Christian church *(right)*.

IN 609 THE ROMAN CATHOLIC pope Boniface IV received permission from the government in Constantinople to consecrate (declare sacred) the Pantheon as a Christian church. The pope lives in Rome and is the head of the Roman Catholic Church.

Christians worship only one god. The previous Romans had worshiped many gods. Thus, before the Pantheon could be used as a Christian church, the Christians wanted all the symbols of the old Roman religion removed. Pope Boniface IV had most of the Pantheon's ornamentation stripped away. Most important, he had the statues of the gods removed and destroyed.

The Pantheon's new name was Santa Maria ad Martyres (Saint Mary among the Martyrs). By consecrating the Pantheon as a Christian church, Pope Boniface IV saved the building from ruin, because as a church it received regular maintenance. The inside was cleaned out, drains were cleared, and vines and trees were removed.

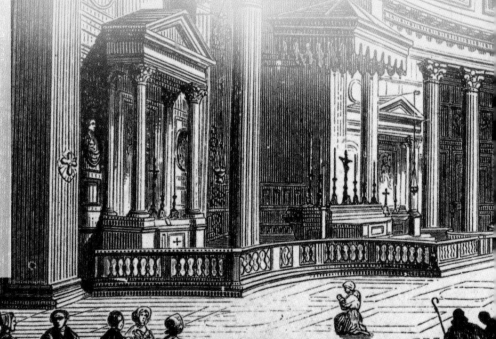

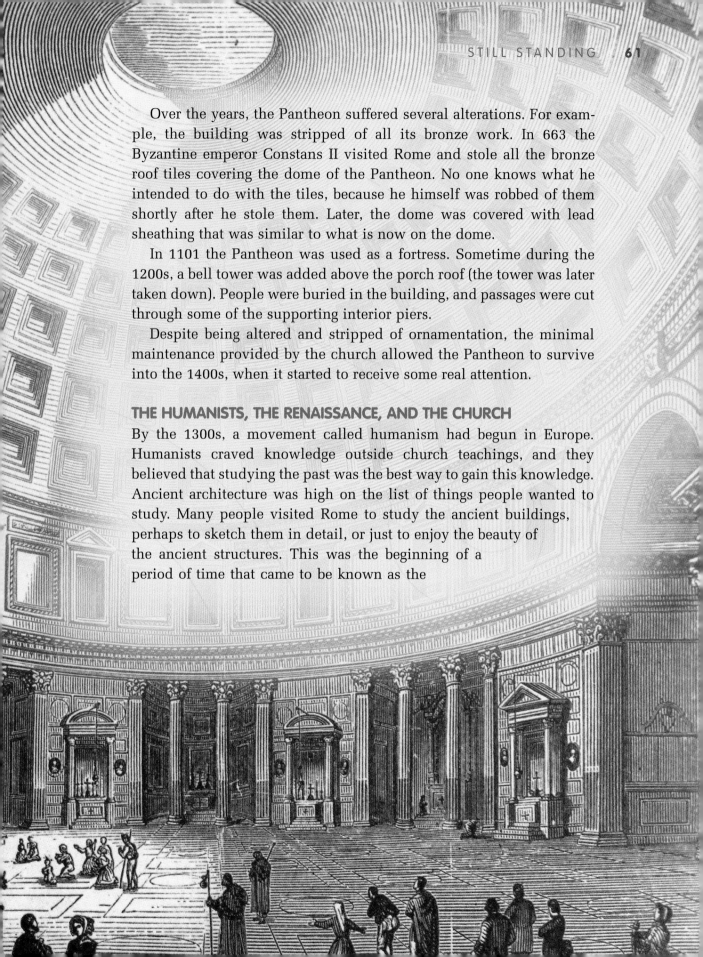

Over the years, the Pantheon suffered several alterations. For example, the building was stripped of all its bronze work. In 663 the Byzantine emperor Constans II visited Rome and stole all the bronze roof tiles covering the dome of the Pantheon. No one knows what he intended to do with the tiles, because he himself was robbed of them shortly after he stole them. Later, the dome was covered with lead sheathing that was similar to what is now on the dome.

In 1101 the Pantheon was used as a fortress. Sometime during the 1200s, a bell tower was added above the porch roof (the tower was later taken down). People were buried in the building, and passages were cut through some of the supporting interior piers.

Despite being altered and stripped of ornamentation, the minimal maintenance provided by the church allowed the Pantheon to survive into the 1400s, when it started to receive some real attention.

THE HUMANISTS, THE RENAISSANCE, AND THE CHURCH

By the 1300s, a movement called humanism had begun in Europe. Humanists craved knowledge outside church teachings, and they believed that studying the past was the best way to gain this knowledge. Ancient architecture was high on the list of things people wanted to study. Many people visited Rome to study the ancient buildings, perhaps to sketch them in detail, or just to enjoy the beauty of the ancient structures. This was the beginning of a period of time that came to be known as the

Renaissance. The word *renaissance* means "rebirth," or "revival," and that's exactly what this period was. Sciences, history, literature, and arts such as architecture received renewed interest. By the 1400s, the Pantheon in particular was receiving a lot of attention from would-be architects and other students of history and art.

The Catholic Church gave Rome a real boost during the Renaissance because several popes wanted to make Italy, and Rome specifically, the center of civilization once again. Rome became a magnet, attracting visitors from all over Europe—even the world. Pope Nicholas V was very interested in the Pantheon, visiting it several times and even engraving his coat of arms and titles on several of the lead sheets covering the dome.

Michelangelo, the great painter, sculptor, and architect, visited the Pantheon in the early 1500s. Although not easily impressed, Michelangelo was amazed by the building. He pronounced it to be of "angelic and not human design."

As interest in preserving the past grew, people began to demand that the government provide better upkeep for ancient buildings, especially for the Pantheon, which was the best-preserved ancient Roman building. In 1515 Pope Leo X appointed the painter Raphael as his superintendent of antiquities. Raphael set about preparing a report on the state of ancient monuments. He had all of them measured and studied in

A sketch of the Pantheon by Raphael

detail, with an eye toward how they might be restored and maintained. It appears that Raphael was quite taken with the Pantheon, since he asked to be buried in it. His tomb is still located within the building.

Anybody who seriously studied the past couldn't help but notice the Pantheon. During the Renaissance, the Pantheon became known as the most beautiful building ever built, and architects began to adapt its design for their own buildings.

ANDREA PALLADIO

Andrea Palladio was an Italian architect who spent several years in Rome during the 1540s and 1550s. During that time, he studiously sketched the Pantheon and other ancient Roman monuments, and published some books on those monuments.

During Palladio's career as an architect, he built nearly fifty buildings: churches, villas, palaces, and civic structures, all of them in northern Italy. He never directly copied the Pantheon, but he studied it so thoroughly that its design influenced nearly every one of his buildings.

People adored Palladio's designs. They were elegant and stately. He managed to capture the grandeur of the Pantheon's enclosed space in nearly everything he designed. Because of Palladio's influence, Pantheon-like buildings became the accepted style for many important buildings. Domed structures with classical porches began showing up in public architecture.

Andrea Palladio popularized principles of Roman architecture in the sixteenth century.

By the 1600s, Palladio's books were available throughout Europe, and his designs were widely known. Other architects picked up Palladio's books on the Pantheon and his own designs and freely used them.

THE SEVENTEENTH CENTURY TO THE PRESENT

In the seventeenth century, two bell towers were added to the Pantheon by the architect and sculptor Gian Bernini. The towers were nicknamed the ass's ears because of their ugliness and were later removed. Also in the seventeenth century, Pope Alexander VII had the left side of the porch rebuilt after it collapsed.

Two bell towers, added to the Pantheon in the seventeenth century and nicknamed the ass's ears, were still there in the early nineteenth century.

Meanwhile, the Pantheon was becoming a source of architectural inspiration throughout Europe and other parts of the world. Replicas showed up all over England, France, and Germany. Some replicas were actually called the Pantheon. All of them, though, were smaller than Hadrian's Pantheon. In the 1800s, the basic design of the Pantheon crossed the Atlantic. Thomas Jefferson, the third president of the United States, was a bit like Hadrian. He was a great statesman who was also interested in culture, history, the arts, and architecture. He designed Monticello, his home in Virginia, after the Pantheon. He went on, designing the library at the University of Virginia (which he also founded) the same way. Jefferson was fascinated by the Pantheon and loved to design domed structures with classical porches.

Nonarchitects appreciated the Pantheon's beauty as well. In 1819 the famous poet Percy Bysshe Shelley commented on "the perfection of its proportions," calling the Pantheon "the visible image of the universe."

The Pantheon became the accepted architectural design for many government buildings. Likewise, many churches have been built using the Pantheon's design.

Why did this architectural design endure for nearly two thousand years? The key to the Pantheon's success as an architectural design doesn't lie in any one factor; it lies in a variety of factors.

One factor is the symbolism of the dome. Hadrian's architects took the imagined shape of the cosmos and put it into concrete form. In capturing the permanence and perfection of the heavens, the dome also captured a sense of beauty and security that everyone can appreciate—not just ancient Romans. When people stand in the rotunda of the Pantheon, they are filled with awe. People have wanted to duplicate it for that reason.

Another reason for the endurance of the Pantheon's design is that it has been adopted by countless groups of authority so it has remained well known. It is a universal design that isn't associated with any one church or any one government. Democratic governments, tyrant kings, pagan cults, and Christian churches have all used domes with temple fronts as symbols of their authority. Most official buildings in existence—state capitols, libraries, museums, and more—take their design from Roman architecture, and frequently the buildings are based specifically on the Pantheon.

The American president Thomas Jefferson designed Monticello, his home in Virginia, after the Pantheon.

COMPUTERS AND THE PANTHEON

Much information about the Pantheon comes from computers. By taking what is already known—such as the density of the concrete—and entering it as data into a computer, scholars have been able to learn more about how the Pantheon stays up. A lot of what we know has been gained by using what's called three-dimensional, finite-element computer modeling.

When information is put into the computer and a computer model is created, scholars can test the model for different things, such as how much hoop stress the dome produces. They can change various characteristics of the Pantheon in the computer model, to see how the building would fare if it were built differently. For example, in one test they found that the lighter concrete aggregates used in the dome are indeed very effective in reducing stress on the building. If the heavier aggregates of the rotunda wall were used in the whole dome, the stresses would have almost doubled.

It's hard for the findings to be exact, because some of the data is based on estimates. But computers are still providing a lot of new information about the Pantheon.

The thinkers and artists of the Renaissance were crucial to the popularity of the Pantheon's design. Before the Renaissance, many Romans and other visitors to the Pantheon had been amazed by the huge dome staying up with no signs of support. They called it the "house of devils" and believed the dome stayed up because of evil demons. But the Renaissance changed the way architecture was studied and transformed the way people thought about the Pantheon. The temple went from being a pagan wonder to a magnificent building in the public's eye. It then became an incredible architectural and engineering feat, designed by a real person—even though no one knew who that person (or people) was.

VISITING THE PANTHEON

The Pantheon is still a church and still sits on its original site, but modern Rome has grown up around it. The forecourt is gone. The busy city has taken up the open space that once surrounded the building. It's still a very important landmark in Rome and is open to the general public.

The building is still lit only by natural sunlight through the oculus of the dome. As Earth rotates, the light inside the rotunda changes. Rain still falls inside.

Even though scholars have a good idea of what the Pantheon's

THE STOLEN BRONZE

We know what happened to some sections of the Pantheon's bronze work. We even know where some of it is. In the 1620s, Pope Urban VIII removed at least 200 tons (181 metric tons) of bronze from the support system of the porch roof. Two hundred tons is roughly the weight of four hundred compact-size automobiles. Urban VIII cast the bronze into eighty cannons. Still later, the bronze in the cannons was recast yet again, and used for the canopy *(right)* over the main altar in Saint Peter's Basilica in Rome—where it can still be seen.

Urban VIII did have respect for the Pantheon. In 1632 he put an inscription at the back of the Pantheon porch, high on the wall, just to the right of the great bronze entrance doors. It reads, in part, "The Pantheon, the most celebrated edifice in the whole world."

interior looked like—statues, gilded rosettes in each coffer, and all the rest—no one has ever restored the lost decorations. And although Roman concrete is amazingly durable, after nearly two thousand years the dome and the foundation of the Pantheon have developed cracks. But because the cracks do not appear to be structurally dangerous, no one has attempted to repair them.

Without the repairs, even without the decorations, the Pantheon is still a beautiful space. It was a great building feat in A.D. 128. Nearly two thousand years later, it is still one of the great building feats of the world. Its symbolism is as strong now as it ever was. It is still a symbol of the heavens and of authority. And the Pantheon is a massive symbol of a lost era. It represents the great Roman Empire at the height of its powers, when the universe seemed glorious and perfect.

Source Notes

Acknowledgments for Quoted Material: pp. 14, 56 (bottom), 57, as quoted in Anthony R. Birley, *Hadrian: The Restless Emperor* (London and New York: Routledge, 1997); pp. 17, 56 (top), as quoted in William L. MacDonald, *The Architecture of the Roman Empire: An Introductory Study* (New Haven, CT and London: Yale University Press, 1982); pp. 62, 64, as quoted by William L. MacDonald, *The Pantheon: Design, Meaning, and Progeny* (Cambridge, MA: Harvard University Press, 1976).

Selected Bibliography

Adam, Jean-Pierre. *Roman Building: Materials and Techniques.* Bloomington and Indianapolis, IN: University Press, 1994.

Allen, Edward. *How Buildings Work: The Natural Order of Architecture.* New York and Oxford: Oxford University Press, 1995.

Birley, Anthony. *Hadrian: The Restless Emperor.* London and New York: Routledge, 1997.

Connolly, Peter, and Hazel Dodge. *The Ancient City: Life in Classical Athens and Rome.* Oxford, England: Oxford University Press, 1998.

De Fine Licht, Kjeld. *The Rotunda in Rome: A Study of Hadrian's Pantheon.* Copenhagen, Denmark: Jutland Archeological Society Publications, 1968.

de la Croix, Horst, Richard G. Tansey, and Diane Kirkpatrick. *Gardner's Art Through the Ages.* 8th Ed. San Diego, CA: Harcourt Brace Jovanovich, 1986.

MacDonald, William L. *The Architecture of the Roman Empire.* New Haven, CT and London: Yale University Press, 1982.

————. *The Pantheon.* Cambridge, MA: Harvard University Press, 1976.

Mainstone, Rowland. *Developments in Structural Form.* Oxford: Architectural Press, 1998.

Mark, Robert, editor. *Architectural Technology up to the Scientific Revolution: The Art and Structure of Large-Scale Buildings.* Cambridge, MA: The MIT Press, 1995.

Mark, Robert. *Light, Wind, and Structure: The Mystery of the Master Builders.* Cambridge, MA: The MIT Press, 1990.

Further Reading and Websites

Barghusen, Joan. *Daily Life in Ancient and Modern Rome.* Minneapolis, MN: Runestone Press, 1999.
This colorful and fact-filled book combines descriptions of daily life and important historical events. Learn about Roman religious life, entertainment, class divisions, and the military through the ages.

Burrell, Roy, and Peter Connolly. *The Romans.* Oxford, England: Oxford University Press, 1991.
Junior-high readers will find a wealth of information and colorful illustrations on Roman history, including conversations with ancient Romans.

Day, Nancy. *Your Travel Guide to Renaissance Europe.* Minneapolis, MN: Runestone Press, 2001.
Take a journey to Renaissance Europe with the help of this awesome book. Wipe your nose on your sleeve, visit Leonardo da Vinci's studio, eat roasted stag, and don't forget your perfume (there may not be a place to take a bath).

The Editors of Time-Life Books. *Rome: Echoes of Imperial Glory.* Alexandria, VA: Time-Life Books, 1994.
This book explores ancient Rome through the findings of archeologists and other scientists. Learn more about the life of the emperor Hadrian, who oversaw the building of the Pantheon.

MacDonald, William. *The Pantheon.* Cambridge, MA: Harvard University Press, 1976.
This book for advanced readers provides information on the Pantheon from the time of its construction to its influence on architects today.

WGBH Educational Foundation. Building Big. 2000.
<http://www.pbs.org/wgbh/buildingbig/index.html> (January 24, 2002).
Click on "Domes" to find your way to the Pantheon.

Woods, Michael, and Mary B. Woods. Ancient Construction. Minneapolis: Runestone Press, 2000.
In the chapter on ancient Rome, discover how Romans invented concrete to aid in their construction of huge structures such as the Pantheon and the Colosseum.

Index

Lesley A. DuTemple has written more than a dozen books for young readers, including many award-winning titles such as her biography *Jacques Cousteau*, winner of the National Science Teachers Association/Children's Book Council Outstanding Science Trade Books for Children. After graduating from the University of California, San Diego, she attended the University of Utah's Graduate School of Architecture, where she concentrated in design and architectural history. The creator of the **Great Building Feats** series, she believes, "There's a human story behind every one of these building feats, and those stories are just as amazing as the projects themselves."

Photo Acknowledgments

All attempts have been made to contact the copyright holder(s) of the images in this book. If your image appears without proper credit, please contact Lerner Publishing Group.

The images in this book are used with the permission of: Superstock, p. 1; © Scott Gilchrist/Archivision, pp. 2–3, 4–5, 18, 40, 42–43, 44, 65; © Bettman/CORBIS, p. 6; © Nimatallah/Art Resource, NY, p. 8; © The British Museum, pp. 8–9; © Alinari/Art Resource, NY, pp. 10–11, 54 (left), 55; © Scala/Art Resource NY, pp. 11, 16, 54 (right), 62; © Réunion des Musées Nationaux/Art Resource, p. 14; © The Art Archive, pp. 16–17, 47; © Werner Forman/Art Resource, NY, pp. 21, 24; © Historical Picture Archive/CORBIS, pp. 26–27, 64; © Steve Strickland/Visuals Unlimited, Inc., p. 29; Van der Heyden Collection/Independent Picture Service, pp. 30, 34, 39, 46, 67; © Vanni Archive/CORBIS, p. 32; © Gianni Dagli Orti/CORBIS, p. 33; © Mimmo Jodice/CORBIS, p. 36; © Eric Lessing/Art Resource NY, p. 50; © North Wind Pictures, pp. 52–53, 60, 63; © Stock Montage, p. 57; © American Academy in Rome, Fototecta Unione, presso Accademia, via A. Masine, p. 58; © Ronald Sheridan/Ancient Art & Architecture Collection, pp. 60–61.

Maps and diagrams by Laura Westlund, pp. 13, 20, 23, 31, 35, 38, 41, 48, back cover. Diagram on p. 35 taken from a scheme devised by Emmanuel Viollet-le-Duc.

Cover photo is by © Stock Montage.